Goal Achieving Tools:
GOD'S TEAMS and More!

Frances Marx

Published by
JFM Integrity

© 2018 Frances Marx

Published by:
JFM Integrity
6515 Tarawa Dr.
Sarasota, Fl. 34241
E-mail: yoursuccessadvocate@gmail.com

All rights reserved. No part of this book may be reproduced or transmitted in any form or by any means including, but not limited to, electronic or mechanical, photocopying, recording, or my any information storage and retrieval system without written permission from the publisher except for the inclusion of brief quotations in review.

Author: Frances Marx
Graphic Designer: Frances Marx
Editor: 3 Strands Creations
Summary: **Goal achieving tools and techniques**

978-0-9916516-3-4

1. Goal Setting, Goal Achieving, Christian, Self-help, Personal Development, Success, Writing, Journal

For current information about releases by Frances Marx or for speaking engagement requests,
E-mail: yoursuccessadvocate@gmail.com
Printed in the United States of America

TABLE OF CONTENTS

ACKNOWLEDGMENT 4

INTRODUCTION 5

HOW TO USE GOAL ACHIEVING TOOLS 6

BLESSING 7

PART I - GOAL SETTING AND ACHIEVING 8

PART II – SUCCESSFUL CHAPTERS OF MY LIFE 15

    1. Going to College! 16
    2. Now What? 18
    3. A New Awakening 19
    4. Creating Something New 21
    5. Avoiding the Pain 23
    6. Painting 25
    7. Home Schooling 26
    8. A New Beginning 27
    9. Becoming an Author 29
    10. Answer to prayer 30

PART III – GOD'S TEAMS defined 32

PART IV – GOAL ACHIEVING WORK SHEETS 34

FOR MORE INFORMATION 118

ABOUT THE AUTHOR 119

ACKNOWLEDGMENT

I want to thank God for always being there for me – to love me, protect me, help guide, and teach me. I thank you, God, for Your faithfulness and everlasting love. Thank you for being my inspiration for all that I do.

I want to thank my husband, John, for being my greatest encourager. You love me more than I could ever imagine being loved. I appreciate your wisdom, guidance, encouragement and support in all God asks me to do. I appreciate your honesty in reviewing all that I propose to do. Without your input and encouragement, this book as well as many other good things I have done, would not have been accomplished.

Thank you to all my family and friends who encouraged me in my efforts and helped me with their suggestions and ideas.

> *"In whatever you do, whether in word or deed, do it all in the name of the Lord Jesus, giving thanks to God the Father through Him."*
> *- Colossians 3:17*

Goal Achieving Tools:
GOD'S TEAMS and More

INTRODUCTION

How often have you set goals, just to see them fail? How often have you created New Year's resolutions and then forgot what they were by the beginning of February? If you have had those experiences, you are like most of us. But it doesn't have to be like that anymore. You are holding in your hands, a book that includes all the tools you need to accomplish your most desired goals. By using these tools, if you are ready to put in the effort, you will be successful.

I have studied goal setting techniques for many years, and while I was teaching a dual enrollment "Introduction to Psychology" class to high school students, I decided to require the students to set a goal they could accomplish within nine weeks. I knew the familiar goal setting acronyms, but I wanted to offer them something different that would encompass every area of setting and achieving goals. I prayed about it and came up with the acronym "GOD'S TEAMS". I am excited about this because, although the sample is small, thus far everyone who has tried the GOD'S TEAMS system, has been successful in achieving their goals. Here are some of their comments:

"The GOD'S TEAMS goal achieving tool was very effective in my personal experience. It's a great way to organize your thoughts and build a plan of action to help achieve your goals in a Christ honoring manner." – Josh H. - High school student

"GOD'S TEAMS was a helpful project that helped me understand what I needed to do, not because it was an easy goal achieving tool, but because it made me survey, understand, and work through my goal to achieve it." – Alissa L. - High school student

"The GOD'S TEAMS plan helped me build confidence in myself I didn't know I had, about math. Math has always been a BIG struggle for me since grade school. Not knowing how to study played a big part too. I am glad GOD'S TEAMS found its way to me. It has been a great help to get me on track to earn my high school equivalency diploma." – Whitney D. - Adult student

"All too often we become distracted by the urgent instead of carrying out God's plan for us. The GOD'S TEAMS goal achieving system has helped me set priorities, establish a plan and evaluate my progress. I would highly recommend it to anyone who is serious about accomplishing her goals." – Chris B. – Author

How to Use
Goal Achieving Tools: GOD'S TEAMS and More!

Goal Achieving Tools: GOD'S TEAMS and More! is organized in an easy to use format.

- Part I is an overview of goal setting and achieving – this is a must read.

- Part II is a collection of situations from my life in which I was able to be successful by using the tools described.

- Part III is the GOD'S TEAMS acronym described.
    1. Please start with the final S – seek God,
    2. then go to the top G – set goals. You do not have to do the components of the other letters in order, but you must include all of them in the goal achieving system.
    3. Once you set your goal, you should continue to evaluate your progress and adjust your plan as needed until you reach your goal.

- Part IV is composed of GOD'S TEAMS goal achieving work-sheets – a tool by which you can create and accomplish your own goals. To help inspire you, at the top of each work-sheet is an inspirational quote.

"Commit to the Lord whatever you do, and He will establish your plans."
- Proverbs 16:3 (NIV)

Blessing

I believe that each chapter of my life has prepared me for the next. When I was experiencing each season of my life, that time seemed like the greatest ever. Then God would open a new chapter that was even better than the last. I don't know where the Lord will lead next, but I do know that I have been blessed my entire life with careers that I have loved and through which I have grown.

Reflecting on my life has given me a desire to help others achieve the successes they desire in their own lives. Although I can do this through my work, I would like to encourage more people. With that end in mind, I have written <u>Goal Achieving Tools: GOD'S TEAMS and More!</u>

As you read about my various life situations, may you be encouraged to know that when you put God first in your life, He will help you with every circumstance. Proverbs 3:6 describes this well. *"In everything you do, put God first, and He will direct you and crown your efforts with success."* (The Living Bible) My hope is that as you take and use the advice given in this book, you too will find fulfillment in your life. May God bless your efforts.

> *"In everything you do, put God first, and He will direct you and crown your efforts with success."*
> **- Proverbs 3:6 (The Living Bible)**

Part 1

Goal Setting and Achieving

Part I

Goal Setting and Achieving

I've studied goal setting and tried a myriad of methods. But no matter the season of life or the technique, I fell short. Why? What was the problem? Intellectually, I know what I should be doing, but I don't do it. Is part of the problem a spiritual rather than natural problem? In Romans 7:15, Paul says, *"I do not understand what I do. For what I want to do I do not do, but what I hate I do." (NIV)*

Reflecting on my life and the times I did achieve relative greatness, in my life sphere, I realized that certain concepts consistently fell into place; and they were always the same. So why couldn't I maintain the process in every area of my life? When I pursued a goal, it was as if I were running a race. I ran to win, I won, and then I rested on my laurels until the next chapter of my life. Why not keep going? I am still not totally sure. The truth of the matter is that you cannot fulfill the call God has on your life unless you keep trying. Hence, anytime you feel discouraged or defeated, you know that this is not God's plan for your life. So, you have an opportunity to choose. Rest on your laurels or keep on persevering for God's purpose.

I identified three things that contributed to my inability to accomplish all my goals on a steady basis:

- One was a lack of intentionality. Living my life intentionally took work. It paid off in tremendous benefits, but it was still work.
- Second was failing to look for the root of what was hindering me. What were the obstacles that stopped me? Were they real concrete obstacles, or obstacles that I created in my mind? It is vital that you reflect on the possible roots of the things that hinder your success.
- Third was that often, pride got in the way.

Frequently, I would get burned out, working hard on a project, feeling as if I were the only one doing all the work. I'm sure some of you have felt that way in your own lives – whether at home, at work or at church. The problem is that if you are consistently getting burned out, it means that you are trying to do everything in your own power rather than relying on God and those he sends to assist you. If you are in this position, as I have been, you are practicing the sin of pride. In several places, the Bible describes pride as a sin.

"The kind of pride the Bible condemns is a pride that puts ourselves first, and leaves God out of the picture. When that happens, we take credit for everything we accomplish, and we live only to please ourselves. This is why pride is at the root of almost every other sin." – billygraham.org The Bible says in James 4:6, *"God resists the proud and gives grace to the humble hearted."* Once I realized that this verse was

real, I did everything possible to become humble before God and let go of the ungodly pride that had been a ruling force in my life.

As a young woman, I was somewhat competitive, but as I have matured as a person and as a person of faith, I no longer feel the need to compete with others. My focus now is to love God, love others, and love myself. If I can do that, everything will fall into place, so I work to be the best I can be in those three areas of life.

I spoke earlier about the consistent concepts that helped me succeed. Let's review them here. They can be summarized as a four-letter acronym: PPPW (Pray, Picture, Ponder, Work)

1. *Pray.* Once I accepted Christ as my Savior, God as my Father, and the Holy Spirit as my Helper, Teacher, Guide and Counselor, I understood the importance of asking for His help and guidance in everything. Looking back on my life, before my acceptance, I realized that from the time I was baptized as an infant, God was with me; protecting me and leading me as much as I would allow Him to. Although I was rarely aware of His presence, at this stage of my life I can see that He was always there. Now, when I feel as if I need to make a change, I ask Him first and follow His lead.
2. *Picture.* Each time, envisioning my goal began with a desire to do something, avoid something, or create a solution to a problem.
3. *Ponder.* I would take time to think about what I wanted to do, what I would have to do to get there, and how I could be successful. I wondered what would make me stand out from the crowd or why people would want to use my services.
4. *Work.* After pondering, and coming up with an answer, I would relentlessly pursue achieving the goal.

"Be Faithful in small things because it is in them that your strength lies."
– Mother Teresa

The Art of Pondering©

Pondering (to think over carefully) is such a crucial piece to accomplishing your goals, that I dedicated a part of my previous book, My Success Journal: A Guided Tour on the Journey to Self-Discovery, to pondering. Because I believe that pondering is becoming a lost art, I have included it in this book also.

What is pondering? Making time to stop and think, on a deep level. If you need to, make an appointment with yourself. Pondering is an intentional activity. If you don't purpose to make it a habit in your life, you will, most likely, relegate it only to times when a situation or emergency forces you to stop and think. If you are not intentional about pondering, when you think, it will probably be on a shallow level. The rest of the time will be spent keeping busy with the affairs of this life, being swept along by the current of life's demands.

How do you ponder? Make and take the time to think about the following:

1. About yourself:
   A. How can you better yourself?
   B. Do you accept responsibility for your actions and decisions?
   C. Do you take others' needs and well-being into consideration?
   D. Do you do what needs to be done in a timely fashion?
   E. Are you dependable?
   F. Do you have integrity?
   G. In your thoughts, on what do you focus?
   H. Are you progressing toward your goals, or are you just keeping busy?
   I. Are you accomplishing, or just participating in many activities?
   J. What are your interests? Examine your behavior to see where you spend your free time the most to get an accurate answer.
   K. In what do you excel? Think about times in which you felt happy about your accomplishment or times when people pointed out that you did a great job or that you were the best in a particular area.
2. About your future:
   A. What makes you happy?
   B. In what areas are you successful?
   C. How can you use your strengths to help others?
   D. How can you use your strengths to make a living?
   E. What would be your best career choice?
   F. What would you want to do with your life if you knew you could not fail?
   G. What characteristics would you like your future spouse to exhibit?
   H. What can you offer to your workplace and to relationships?
   I. What is stopping you from achieving your goals?
3. About others:
   A. How does your behavior affect others?
   B. What can you do to help someone else?
   C. How can you make someone else's life easier?

        D. How can you show respect, honor, and/or caring to someone?
    4. What are your strengths and weaknesses?
        A. Academically
        B. Physically
        C. Socially
        D. Spiritually
        E. Emotionally
    5. Choosing a career that best suits you:
        A. Do your thoughts and behaviors influence the achievement of your goals?
        B. What are your goals?
        C. How will you achieve those goals?
        D. How will you provide for yourself and your family after high school/college?
        E. Match your visions and dreams for the future with your strengths and interests to find possible career choices.
        F. Do your research concerning each career.

Where will you ponder? You can ponder anywhere you find yourself with a few free moments. In addition, you can find or create a designated quiet place to ponder.

Who should ponder? Everyone

Why is pondering important? Pondering is crucial because if you don't take time to:

- *Analyze* (to examine methodically),
- *Synthesize* (to produce something new by combining separate elements), and
- *Evaluate* (to examine and judge),

which are all higher levels of thinking, you will be subject to living your lives responding to circumstances and outside influences rather than being true to yourselves by being intentional in your thoughts and actions. Henry David Thoreau said, *"The mass of men lead lives of quiet desperation."* If you do not stop to think, it will be hard to live life deliberately and to fulfill your life's purposes.

After pondering, I would find that the ideas would swirl around in my head. There were grandiose visions and dreams, but no concrete steps or organization that would take me from vision to reality.

The solution to that problem was journaling. It became an essential aspect of my growing process. When I journaled,

- I clarified ideas and made plans for achieving them.
- I also used the journal to see if I was moving in the right direction or remaining stagnant. After writing for a month or so, I would review where I was in the present versus where I had been a month prior. If I was reacting and behaving in the same way, I knew I needed to evaluate my plan, toss out was wasn't working and adjust with a new plan.

- In addition to seeing what did not work in my life, I was encouraged by my successes – no matter how small.
- Journaling really helped to keep me honest with myself. You may think that it is easy to be honest with yourself, but I have found from experience that it is easiest to deceive yourself.

I will give you two examples from my own life. When I was a teenager, I loved to dance, and every weekend our youth group had a dance. We would meet at someone's house or we would rent a facility and hire a band. It was a great experience. As an adult, not realizing that I had changed, I told myself that I loved to dance and that the only reason I hadn't danced in years was because my ex-husband did not like to dance. When he left, and I was single, I suppose I wanted to go back to that happy place in my life. I kept telling myself that same old lie, "I love to dance". I did not want to go to a bar, so I would look up other community places I could go to dance. I would even write down the dates and times. I did that for the seven years I was single. When I met my current husband, I told him I loved to dance, and he took me dancing a few times even though he was not really a fan. After we were married I reflected on my dancing days while I was single. I realized that where I spent my time was really where my heart was. Then the lightbulb moment came, and I became fully aware that the entire time I was single and had opportunity to dance, I never went dancing. What I did do with any spare time I had was to go to church, Christian workshops, and read the Bible; basically, my heart was really into seeking the Lord, it was not on the dance floor. That was a refreshing revelation.

The second lie I told myself was that I hated detail work. I don't know where that came from, but I always said it. Finally, my husband, who often questions things that don't seem real, asked me why I always said that I hated detail work. He said that for the entire time he has known me, everything I did centered on doing detail work, that I did it well and seemed to take pleasure in my accomplishments. In fact, he was correct. When I looked back at my life from an objective point of view, I realized that rather than hating detail work, I had embraced it and enjoyed it.

It is imperative that you become aware of how you speak to yourself. James Allen wrote a book entitled <u>As a Man Thinketh</u> in which he explores the power of your thoughts in relation to determining the outcome of your life. It is a small book, easy to read, with a powerful and true message. Along those same lines, the following quote is attributed to many authors over several years, and it includes some basic truths you can apply to your life.

> *"Watch your thoughts, they become your words;*
> *watch your words, they become your actions;*
> *watch your actions, they become your habits;*
> *watch your habits, they become your character;*
> *watch your character, for it becomes your destiny."*

The Bible also stresses the importance of being intentional in your thoughts. Philippians 4:8-9 states, *"Finally, brothers and sisters, whatever is true, whatever is noble, whatever is right, whatever is pure, whatever is lovely, whatever is admirable, - if anything is excellent or praiseworthy – think about such things. Whatever you have learned or received or heard from me or seen in me – put into practice. And the God of peace will be with you." (NIV)*

As you consider your thoughts, examine your belief system. Do you believe that you are who you are and can never change? If this is the case, be careful. You may be falling prey to a victim mentality, even if you don't consciously see yourself in that light. You demonstrate a victim mentality when you believe that you have no power to change your life. You become a victim of your circumstances, your past choices or things that have happened to you in the past.

The Bible does not support that idea. Romans 8:37 states, "*No, in all these things we are more than conquerors through Him who loved us.*" (NIV) Remember that your circumstances do not define you. They are things that happen to you but are not who you are. Once you realize this, you can work on changing your thoughts by reminding yourself of what God has said about who you, His creation, are. In Ephesians 2:10 *"For we are God's handiwork, created in Christ Jesus, to do good works, which God prepared in advance for us to do"* (NIV).

Jeremiah 29:11 states, "*For I know the plans I have for you,"* declares the Lord, *"plans to prosper you and not to harm you, plans to give you hope and a future*" (NIV). God created you to be a creative, intelligent human being who can grow in wisdom. He did not create you to be a stagnant being. God has big plans for you. It is up to you to decide to participate.

After pondering and journaling, you can become more aware of where you are now, what you need to change, where you want to go, and how you will get from where you are to where you want to go.

Concerning myself, I have had several careers. I see each one as a chapter of growth in my life, leading to my being able to positively impact others in my current jobs as well as write this book. For those of you who are interested, I have included some of the chapters of my life in this book so that you can see how the process works. If you would prefer to start working on achieving your own goals, please go to page 34 to begin your journey of learning more about yourself and accomplishing your goals. May God bless your efforts.

"For we are God's handiwork, created in Christ Jesus, to do good works, which God prepared in advance for us to do."
- Ephesians 2:10 (NIV)

Part II

Successful Chapters of My Life

Part II

Successful Chapters of My Life

1. Going to College!

In eighth grade, I made a poor decision. I decided that I did not want to do my homework; and I didn't. Then, as the end of the school year approached, I realized that if I did not do the minimal amount of work required, I would not graduate. I stayed home for three days and worked non-stop to complete all the assignments that had been due. I found grace that my teachers accepted my work and I graduated, albeit grades in all my subjects were Ds.

At that time, before a student enrolled in high school, their records were reviewed, and the student was placed into one of two tracks in high school – college bound, or non-college bound. When the administrators looked at my records, even though my standardized test scores were extremely high, since my grades were barely passing, I was put in the non-college bound track. I took courses like sewing, cooking, typing and all regular classes. I had no honors classes.

During the summer between my freshman and sophomore year, I worked at my father's snack shop style restaurant. I learned that although my father was a genius in the kitchen and could remember every order, even without a written ticket, I could not remember anything pertinent to the situation. This job was his passion, not mine. I would always forget something – water, silverware, etc. One day, at breakfast, I determined that I would remember everything. I was working a U-shaped counter. I took everyone's order, gave them their coffee, cream, napkin, silverware, and water. I was so proud of myself. Then reality hit. My dad started calling out the orders I had given him, and I realized that I did not know which customer was to receive each order.

It was on that day that I decided I needed to do something different with my life. Working in my dad's restaurant, and being young, the customers were kind to me. They left tips even though I did not give excellent service. But I knew that as an adult, that would not be the case. The customers would expect more from me. I knew that I would never go hungry being a waitress, because I could always eat in the restaurant. I also knew that being a terrible waitress would never give me the opportunity to live the life I wanted to live. The problem was that I had no idea what I could do differently.

When I returned to school in the fall, God intervened in the form of my Geometry teacher. She kept me after class one day and asked me why I was enrolled in the kinds of classes I was taking. I told her that I was in them because that was where I had been placed. She said, "You can go to college." I said excitedly, "I can go to college?! Really?" She said, "Yes. You have the ability to go." I was so excited that I had an opportunity to do something other than waitressing, that as soon as I could, I raced down to the counselor's office to see how I could make it happen.

I worked with the counselor to change my junior and senior year schedules to include all the pre-college courses I would need to make me eligible to attend college. The last two years of high school were very challenging, but I did it. I was on my way!

> *"If God is your partner, make your plans BIG!"*
> *– D.L. Moody*

2. Now What?

Now that I was set on a path to go to college, I needed some direction. What course of study would I pursue? Could I earn a living in that field of study? How could I find out? I started in the library. I read all the books I could about discerning your ideal career choices. The bottom line of all these books was "do what you love, and the money will follow". I thought about what I loved. I had an excellent English teacher who led us through the ancient Greek and Roman classics, which I found fascinating. In addition, Physical Education was one of my favorite classes. How could I combine the two? Ancient Greek philosophers believed in a strong mind and a healthy body. I decided I would pursue Physical Education and promote this concept with all my students. I decided on becoming a Physical Education teacher.

I didn't want to go to community college because they did not provide the education I would need. My parents could not afford the private colleges that were in the area, and they would not allow, nor could they afford for me to go away to college. Once again, God intervened.

The University of Illinois, which was in southern Illinois, decided to open a second campus in Chicago, where I lived. U of I at Chicago Circle began offering classes in the fall of my college freshman year. I applied to the College of Physical Education and went in to speak with the head of the department. Although my grades were not high enough for acceptance, my standardized test scores were high, and after my interview, the department chair said that she would take a chance on me. She thought I would do well once I entered college. She believed in me, gave me a chance and I did not let her down. When I graduated, I was on the Dean's list.

This career gave me the ability to do everything I loved at the time and a good salary as well. During the school year, I taught Physical Education in the Chicago High Schools and I taught volleyball and exercise for adults through the Chicago Park District in the evenings. During the summer, I coordinated and taught in the camp programs for middle school students for the Chicago Park District. Years later, when I moved to the suburbs and started my family, I began teaching recreational volleyball and exercise to adults through the local school district in evening classes. Choosing this career was a great first career for me and my family.

> *"Finally, be strong in the Lord and in His mighty power."*
> **- Ephesians 6:10 (NIV)**

3. A New Awakening

I was a stay at home mom with two little girls when I started this next journey. My oldest daughter was around four years old. She had identified all the letters in the alphabet when she was eighteen months old, before she ever heard the alphabet song. She was reading when she was three years old. One of my neighbors, who was very involved in supporting activities for gifted children, told me that my daughter was gifted and that I should go with her to attend meetings sponsored by a parent group called Friends of Gifted and Talented Children (FOGTC). My response was, "How can she be gifted? She is my daughter." Being introduced to this organization was the beginning of a new chapter in my life. I decided to go to the meeting. I found it to be so interesting that I thought to myself, "Even if my daughter is not gifted, I will enjoy going to these meetings just for my personal edification."

I began doing research to learn about gifted children and their possible educational opportunities. I put myself on the mailing lists of every cultural organization in Chicago. I organized trips to take the children and their parents to various venues. After a short time, I created a newsletter called "Broaden Your Horizons" in which I shared some information about gifted children, education, and cultural activities. Eventually, I became president of the group. At the time, we had 40 families from three small school districts represented in our group. I stopped to think about why people would join our group and pay a small fee to cover the expenses for printing the newsletter. I decided that people would come if we offered them something of value that they couldn't get anywhere else. I had started with the newsletter. Then I wrote a booklet about gifted children and their educational options. We gave this booklet to people when they became members of our group.

We had monthly informational meetings. Ultimately, we created a school after school for gifted children and a summer school during which the children could interact with professionals in their fields and participate in fun activities such as art, rocket launching, foreign language, sculpture and theater. Our group lobbied for better opportunities for our gifted children. As part of our lobbying efforts, I interviewed the education professionals in the surrounding eight school districts, and eventually wrote a book comparing the programs for gifted students from the surrounding communities as well as our program. This book was described at the Florida State Conference for Gifted Education as an excellent resource book. In time, our district added monies to support a better program for gifted students. By the time I was ready to resign my position as president, Friends of Gifted and Talented Children had grown into a group of over 300 families representing 13 school districts.

Being involved with FOGTC was a most exciting chapter of my life; filled with personal growth and awareness. I genuinely appreciate having had the opportunity to participate in this experience. During the five years that I was president of the group, I learned so much about myself. I had never really thought of myself as smart or stupid, I just was. At one of the first meetings I attended, the speaker was telling parents, "If your children score in this range on the ACT or SAT, they are in the gifted range." I said to myself, "Wait a minute! I scored higher than that on the tests I took!"

I was around 30 years old and just starting to realize that I might have some unique talents. Through the programs I initiated and my experiences with the group I came to realize that I had leadership qualities; I learned that I had creative ideas and perspectives that no one else had. I was interviewed for the local newspaper and radio station. I discovered that I had something of value to add to others. Basically, I realized that I could be a person of influence for good. At the end of this chapter of my life, I felt I had used every gift I had and used it to the max. It was an exhilarating and life changing experience. Then I moved to Sarasota, Florida to start a new chapter of my life.

> *"Your potential is the sum of all the possibilities God has for your life."*
> *- Charles Stanley*

4. Creating Something New

When I relocated to Sarasota, Florida it was a real adventure. I moved there with my three girls while my husband finished up his work in Chicago. I was immediately offered positions in education and at the library but decided that I wanted to do something altogether different. I felt so empowered by my experiences with Friends of Gifted and Talented Children that I believed I could do anything I set my mind to. My mother had always said, "Where there's a will, there's a way." I believed her.

I decided that I wanted to open my own company. I stopped to think about what I wanted in a business. I wanted one that I could eventually oversee rather than work at, and one that could blossom into an enterprise that my children could take over if they wanted to. Of course, it had to be a money-making proposition also. I started looking at franchises. They were all very expensive – starting at $100,000, and this was over 30 years ago. I did not have nor want to invest that much money.

I talked it over with my dad and uncle, who were both businessmen. They both told me about a pretzel establishment that was very successful in the Chicago area. It seemed like a good fit for my criteria. When I investigated this venture, I discovered that it was part of a conglomerate of businesses. They did not provide franchises. They would open a branch of the company and hire a manager. Because I wanted to be my own boss, I decided to create my own pretzel business. My thinking was that, although this conglomerate had millions of dollars to support their organization, I could work hard and that would make up for my lack of finances. Since I never owned my own retail shop, I spent quite a bit of time researching all that would be involved.

I hired a general contractor to oversee what I was doing and to obtain permits. Then I did everything else that was required to create the business. I negotiated my lease in a mall, I negotiated with and hired all the subcontractors; electricians, plumbers, and a cabinet maker, who built my kiosk. I purchased all the equipment and opened accounts with all my suppliers. I hired an accountant to oversee my financial records. I named my 10'x12' kiosk, Pretzels on Parade.

Initially I sold pretzels and pretzel toppings, cold drinks, coffee, churros and nachos with cheese. I worked very hard because I had to keep my business open during all mall hours, which totaled 80 hours per week at the store. Eventually I was able to hire people to help me so that I could spend more time with my children.

After the first year, I was chosen to be a distributor for the Florida Lottery. The first problem was that I never gambled. To solve that dilemma, I studied the rules and odds of all the games so that I could understand them. The second difficulty that I thought of was, "Why would anyone make a special trip to buy lottery tickets from my business when they could easily buy these tickets when they go grocery shopping or when they stop to get gas?"

As I sat there pondering, the Lord intervened again and gave me a great plan. It was this: If I was friendly, knowledgeable, fast, and accurate, people would buy tickets from me. This idea was like much of what the Lord shares with us. It was simple and powerful, but often not easy. That plan became the foundation of my business. I worked the plan and made sure that my employees did the same, and it worked amazingly well. The mall closed after I had been there for nine years, but by that time I had earned the distinction of being number one in instant ticket sales in three counties and number nine out of 7500 retailers in lottery ticket sales. More importantly, God used my business to minister peace and joy to my customers and to sustain my girls and me during the chapter that was next to come. It would be a painful chapter.

> *"We are all faced with a series of great opportunities brilliantly disguised as impossible situations."*
> *- Chuck Swindoll*

5. Avoiding the Pain

Just before I opened my business, my husband of almost twenty years left my three girls and me. He wanted a divorce. It was a very dark time for all of us. At first, I just sat in my room and cried. Then one night, when I was saying good night to my girls, my oldest daughter said to me, "You know mom, you're just not here for us anymore." Her words cut through my heart like a knife and I knew she was right. It was imperative that I to do something to pull myself together and be a support for my children. I needed a relationship with the Lord, but I didn't know it yet. I went for secular counseling and learned more about myself, my self-talk, and how I could choose to be different. Getting help from a counselor was a good start. What I realized later in the healing process was that you can be in secular counseling for years and get some degree of healing, but God can bring complete healing in a moment, when you let Him. Sometimes I think He takes a little longer, because we are not ready to receive an instantaneous healing. Sometimes he uses what we are going through to strengthen us and draw us closer to Him. Sometimes, when there is no healing, we don't understand why, and that is just the way it is.

Before I opened my business, a neighbor invited me to a Christian women's home party. I went but wasn't interested. She prayed for me to come to the Lord. When my husband first left, another Christian neighbor gave me books about reconciliation with my husband and offered to help me in any way she could. Again, I was not interested. But these two women planted seeds that others would water.

Once again, God intervened. He surrounded me with strong Christians who reflected God's love for me and introduced me to the Triune God – Father, Son, and Holy Spirit. The contractor I hired was a Christian who held Bible studies at his home. He told me about the Lord and invited me to attend. The contractor and his wife were instrumental in teaching me about the character of God. They were faithful to pray for me and every time I called they would pray with me to shore me up and give me the strength I needed. They loved me like God loves me and were able to offer me the support I needed to get started on my path with the Lord. Through my struggles and pain, I was now ready to seek the Lord.

Then I received an incredible gift from God. A woman named Dorothy came to my store. She shuffled up to my kiosk, slammed her hand on the counter and said, "Give me some of that great coffee!" I told her that the specialty coffee shop was behind my kiosk, but she insisted on buying coffee from me. She was 87 years old when I met her, and her blue eyes sparkled and were filled with life and joy. I was hooked. She got my interest. She and I met every day, either at the store or at her house. She taught me about the necessity of forgiveness, the love of God, and having absolute faith. It is incredible to me that God would touch someone's heart in such a way that she would feel compelled to help me - the hurting, hard headed, prideful person that I was - daily for three years. I am humbled to the core by His grace and her willingness to be obedient to the call. Dorothy died when she was ninety and promised to put in a good word for me when she saw the Lord.

My time during and after the divorce was spent seeking healing from the pain for myself and my children by pursuing a relationship with the Lord. It has taken time, and He is not finished with me or my children yet. It is a journey. God's love is what drew me close to Him and the gift of His peace in times of trouble is a gift I treasure deeply.

After approximately five years of seeking the Lord through Bible studies, women's meetings, and attending church, I felt as if I might be interested in dating or possible marriage. This time, I prayed, "Lord, if I am ever to marry again, please bring me a man who loves You more than anything." That was my prayer. God answered that prayer with a man who does love the Lord more than anything and is able to love me and my children like God loves us. We dated for two years and then God gave us a miracle wedding. I am so blessed to be married to him. We will soon be celebrating our 24th wedding anniversary and are even more in love now than when we first married.

From the beginning, people wanted to hear the story of our wedding. Almost a year after our wedding, after much prodding from my customers, I wrote about our miracle wedding in a booklet entitled <u>Mall Order Bride: A True Cinderella Story</u> as an encouragement to others to trust in the Lord and in the power of His might. More than 2,000 people from all over the world have a copy of this story. Years after first publishing the booklet, I would meet people who had the story and they would tell me that they still had <u>Mall Order Bride</u> in a place where their guests could see it. It was interesting that every time I tell people the story, a spirit of joy is present among us. Thank God for the gift of a wonderful wedding and an even better marriage.

> *"You turned my wailing into dancing; You removed my sackcloth and clothed me with joy."*
> *- Psalm 30:11 (NIV)*

6. Painting

One year after we married, the mall closed. The people that worked with me from the Florida Lottery offered to negotiate a new lease on my behalf at a larger mall in town. I thought about it and decided that it was time for a change. I wanted to be available to spend time with my husband, children, and step-children, so I declined their offer. Our children told me about a job opening at our local school for a Physical Education teacher assistant. I thought that was a great idea since that was my background, and that it would be an easy way to transition back into teaching.

I applied for the job and told my husband about it. He asked, "Did you pray about it?" I said, "No". Then he said that if it worked out fine, and if not, I could stay home. After working so hard in the mall, staying home sounded good to me. I prayed about it and went for the interview. They were very interested, but then hired someone in-house to work at the school.

Now that I was home all day and the children were in school. I started deep cleaning the house. That lasted about two months. I wondered what to do next. My husband asked if I would like to help him in his painting contractor business. I took care of the financials, wrote estimates and invoices and learned how to paint, caulk, pull hoses and take care of equipment.

I loved working with my husband. We listened to Christian radio and could discuss topics when they came to mind. It was a wonderful experience that lasted approximately seven years. On the other side of the coin, it was also a lesson in humility. When I first started, I would get frustrated that I couldn't paint or do anything else on the job as well as my husband. I expressed my frustration and anger. Finally, he said, "You are so arrogant! You think you can come in and start painting as well as I do, and I have been working in this profession for over 30 years." I realized he was right, and I stopped judging myself so harshly. He made that easy for me because he was a patient, gentle teacher and I became teachable.

As the years went by, working with my husband, I could see that sometimes the work was taking its toll on my husband. Consequently, as I was painting I would be talking to God. I'd say, "Lord, You gave me an excellent education and I want to be my husband's best helpmate. I believe that You want to use the education You provided to help me help my husband. I just don't know what You would want me to do. I am happy painting here with him, but I think You have something more for me that entails using my education." I would not get the answer to that conversation for about three or four years, but when I received it, it was tremendous. You will read about that in the next two chapters.

7. Home Schooling

When we first married, my husband's daughter was eight years old and going into third grade. There was a problem. In her previous school, the school taught sight reading rather than phonics. She was a sweetheart and almost every month she was awarded student of the month. I thought there was something wrong when I reviewed her standardized test scores. They were very low and yet she was always bringing home papers marked 100% Great Job! Apparently, the teachers had been giving her work that she could do rather than grade level work. So, when we married and switched her schools, the new teacher had to set up a special program to help her get up to speed in reading. Her special program continued from third grade through fifth. Then she went to middle school.

Middle school was so overwhelming for her that one day she asked if I would home school her. I told her that for me to home school her, I would have to give up my life. I assured her that I would be happy to do so if she was going to work hard, but that I would not home school if she was not going to work. She agreed to work, and I started home schooling her.

I found a curriculum that had diagnostic tests and that was not threatening to her. I combined that with the Hooked-on Phonics© program. Once she completed the diagnostics, I created a chart which listed how many lessons she would have to complete to get to grade level by the end of the school year. We worked diligently from October to May. It was very challenging. Many days we were both in tears, but we learned a great deal. I learned to be gentler and she learned how to work hard on her school work. To help us, my husband was in prayer all day while he was at work. Our combined efforts worked. She had moved up two grade levels in reading in seven months and was now reading at grade level. God helped us with everything. She returned to middle school and went on to graduate from high school on the honor roll. She recently returned to school to become a Licensed Practical Nurse. Currently she is the department chair at her nursing facility and oversees wound care. She is an excellent wife and mother of four terrific children. Thank God for His loving grace and faithfulness.

> *"Teach me Your way, Lord, that I may rely on Your faithfulness; give me an undivided heart that I may fear your name."*
> **- Psalm 86:11 (NIV)**

8. A New Beginning

The daughter mentioned in the previous chapter went to one of the county high schools in our town and participated in JROTC (Junior Reserve Officer Training Corps). Toward the end of her freshman year, she was asked to attend a new charter high school which had a focus on leadership training through the JROTC. My husband was concerned that it may not be a good fit for her or even a good school, so he asked me to attend the informational meetings that were being held to inform the public about the school. I went to the first two meetings and thought the school sounded great. When I went to the third meeting, God intervened again!

I came home, and my heart was bursting with excitement! I told my husband that I really wanted to be the guidance counselor for the new school. My husband said, that it sounded like an excellent idea and that I should submit my request, along with my resume and letters of recommendation to the headmaster. I did what my husband suggested. I didn't consider the facts that I did not have the training and certification needed to be a guidance counselor. Also, I hadn't taught for at least fifteen years. I just applied, trusting that if God wanted me to be the guidance counselor, I would be.

On the first day of school, I introduced myself to the headmaster and he welcomed me with open arms. Initially I was hired as a helper. I did many odd jobs around campus. I had so much fun working there. It was great. After a few weeks, the financial officer called me in and told me that they could not keep me because I worked too hard and they could not afford to pay me. Having owned a business myself, I understood that an owner cannot always have all the help he wants. I returned to painting with my husband who said that since God put this desire in my heart, it would eventually happen. A few weeks later, I was rehired as a substitute for three weeks. Then I went back to painting. Toward the end of the school year, I was rehired to be a replacement physical education teacher. At the end of the year, the headmaster told me that I had been approved to be the guidance counselor, starting in the fall, with the caveat that if I didn't return to school and earn my master's degree in guidance and counseling within three years, I would be fired. The school district allowed a three-year window for a temporary certificate.

I had a decision to make. I was 55 years old. I hadn't been in school for over 30 years. I would be working full time while going to school. How could I do all that? Then I remembered my prayer asking God to use my education for His purposes and to enable me to be a best helpmate for my husband. This job would give me an opportunity to work for ten years and help us financially. Also, since I believed that God put this desire in my heart, I knew that He would help me.

Concerning my master's and certification, God helped every step of the way. He brought the right people into my life who would give me the tools and information I needed to succeed. I did earn my master's degree within the three years allotted.

At the beginning of my first year, I sat in my office and started to ponder: "How can I be successful in this position when I have so many different groups to accommodate – administration, staff, parents, and students?" The idea came to me that if I had a servant's heart and did all I could to make each group's life easier, I would be successful. That is what I did, and I was successful.

When I began this career, the school had 267 students and I, as the only guidance counselor, was doing four or five different jobs. When I retired, nine years later, the school enrollment was almost 1,000 and the guidance department had four guidance counselors and a secretary. Rather than several jobs, my main responsibility was to be the director of the guidance department. Becoming the guidance counselor and adding to the success of the school through the services of the guidance department was quite a journey of growth. I worked hard and received many accolades for the work I did. I loved my job!

Then in May of my ninth year, I received a surprise message. I felt very strongly that the Lord said, "Time's up". I was bewildered but believed that I needed to retire because God said, "Time's up". I submitted my letter of resignation and retired. I did not realize it at the time, but two months later, for personal reasons, I would be greatly needed at home. Because of my obedience, I was home when I needed to be. God always prepares the way for us.

> *"I will instruct you and lead you in the way you should go; I will counsel you with My loving eye on you."*
> *- Psalm 32:8 (NIV)*

9. Becoming an Author

I enjoyed retirement for a while. I was exercising more and spending more time with my husband. But something was missing. I felt as if I still had more to offer others, but no venue in which to do so. I thought about my time as a guidance counselor and remembered something I would tell all my students, "Create a 'success journal' in which you record all the good things you do during your time in high school. Then when you are a senior, you will have all the components needed to create an excellent resume." Everyone liked that idea.

I thought, "Why not write a book about keeping a success journal so that I could help other students. Now that I'm retired, I have plenty of time." Unfortunately, I did not know how or where to start. Once again, God intervened. At the Christian bookstore in our town a guest speaker was the president of a Christian book publishing company. She spoke about writing and getting published. Her talk was the impetus I needed to get started. I wrote, "<u>My Success Journal: A Guided Tour on the Journey to Self-Discovery</u>". It was well received, and those who purchased the book on Amazon gave it 5-star reviews. It is still available on Amazon.

My book was used in high school, with troubled youth and with students who had learning disabilities. In addition, I volunteered at a local half-way house and went through the book with women in recovery. I was also invited to speak at an international Christian College Advisors Conference, as well as local empowering women type workshops.

<u>My Success Journal</u> seemed to have a positive impact in every case. I received a report from the teacher of the students with learning disabilities. At their school, someone had committed suicide. The teacher was using <u>My Success Journal</u> with her students and monitoring their entries. Because the students were using the journal to reflect on their reactions and thoughts to the suicide, and because the teacher reviewed their entries, she was able to identify three students who were vulnerable to suicide. The students received the help they needed, and lives were saved.

During this chapter of my life, I learned a great deal about the entire process of writing a book, creating a website and a blog, and successfully marketing the book and myself. I also learned that although my heart was in sharing information and helping people, my passion was not in marketing the book. God had other plans for me for the next season of my life.

> *"This is what the Lord, the God of Israel says, 'Write in a book all the words I have spoken to you.'"*
> *- Jeremiah 30:2 (NIV)*

10.   Answer to Prayer

I was retired and doing things with <u>My Success Journal</u> for approximately three years, but I still felt like there was more for me to do. Furthermore, I wanted to earn more money. One day, I was at lunch with some friends and one of the women had a prayer journal in which she would record prayer requests and then highlight them when they were answered. She asked if anyone had a prayer request. I said yes. My desire was that:

- I would have a job in which I would use all my gifts,
- earn extra money, and
- have no stress.

Everyone chuckled, since it seemed to be a somewhat impossible request. But is anything too hard for God? He had been working on this new plan for years, and now it was coming into fruition. Let me give you some background before I reveal His plans for me.

A few years before I retired, a local Christian school wanted to start a high school. The principal's secretary was the parent of two of the students who attended the charter school at which I worked. She came to me and asked questions about what was needed for the guidance portion of the high school. I loved speaking with her and freely gave her everything I could think of in terms of advice and tools. As her school progressed she used those tools. When she had questions, I was there to answer them. The time came when she decided to change jobs. Another person could take care of the registrar's duties she had, but there was no one for guidance. About two weeks after my prayer request, the question arose; who can take over the guidance duties at our Christian school? The registrar said, "I know Fran Marx is retired, but perhaps she may be interested in a part time position." The principal called me, I interviewed and was hired. An answer to my prayer and theirs. Halleluiah! When God makes the arrangements, everyone wins. I was excited about this new opportunity and thought that God had answered my prayer completely. I was wrong.

Two years prior to this, I had been playing Pickleball at the gym and a woman came up to me. This was the first and only time I saw her. She said that she was a retired guidance counselor and asked if I knew of any part time guidance counselor jobs available. I had never heard of such a thing, and told her no. The next day I was driving past our local vocational school and there was a sign on the marquee which said, "Part time guidance counselor wanted". I thought this might be a sign of some kind, so I applied and interviewed for the job. It was not a good fit for me since it would entail teaching men who were attempting to earn their high school equivalency diploma. The opportunity sounded interesting except for the fact that it was in jail. I don't mind working with people who have problems, but I did not want to work in jail.

Fast forward two years. Two weeks after I accepted the position at the Christian school, I received a call from the county school district asking if I would be interested in working in the inner city to help people earn their high school equivalency diploma and to be a career coach. I thought, "Wow! Working with adults would be an entirely different demographic and I would be using all my gifts."

I agreed and now work the two, part time jobs – one at a Christian school, and one in the inner city. In both positions:

- I use all my gifts,
- earn extra money,
- and have no stress.

I am appreciated in both positions and I am very grateful to have the opportunities to encourage all my students and co-workers. Another answer to prayer. God is awesome!

> *"Because of the Lord's great love, we are not consumed, for His compassions never fail. They are new every morning; great is Your faithfulness."*
> *- Lamentations 3:22-23 (NIV)*

Part III

GOD'S TEAMS Defined

Part III
GOD'S TEAMS© GOAL ACHIEVING SYSTEM

Note: Begin with the final "S" – seek God first and then continue from the top. The steps do not have to be followed in order, but all the steps must be included in your goal achieving process.

G – **Goal** – What do you want to accomplish?

O – **Obstacles** – What is keeping you from achieving your goal?

D - **Draft** a plan to overcome each obstacle that is stopping you from achieving your goal.

S – **Steps** – What small steps do you need to take to accomplish your goal?

T – **Time** – When do you expect to accomplish your goal?

E – **Evaluate** - Are the steps to achieving your goal working? What is working and what is not? What needs to change? What will you do instead?

A – **Adjust** – Make any adjustments needed so that you can successfully achieve your goal.

M – **Measure** - create a goal you can measure and be specific

S – **Seek** God's plan for you in all you do.

Make a new goal each time you accomplish a goal.

What do you want to do next on your path to follow God's plan for you?

Part IV

Goal Achieving Worksheets

Part IV
<u>Goal Achieving Work Sheets</u>

In this section, fill in the answers to the questions to help you achieve your most desired goals.

"Nothing is impossible. The word itself says, 'I'm possible.'"
– Audrey Hepburn

Goal: What do you want to accomplish?
_____
_____

Obstacles: What is keeping you from achieving your goal?
_____
_____
_____

Draft a plan to overcome each obstacle that is stopping you from achieving your goal.
_____
_____
_____
_____
_____
_____

Steps: What small steps do you need to take to accomplish your goal?
_____
_____
_____
_____
_____
_____

Time: When do you expect to accomplish your goal?
_____
_____

Evaluate: Are the steps to achieving your goal working? What is working and what is not? What needs to change? What will you do instead?

_____
_____
_____
_____
_____
_____

Adjust: Make any adjustments needed so that you can successfully achieve your goal. What are these adjustments?

_____
_____
_____
_____

Measure: How will you know when you have achieved your goal? Be specific.

_____
_____
_____

Seek God's plan for you in all you do. After prayer, listening and observing, what is the next goal you believe God has for you?

_____
_____
_____
_____
_____
_____
_____

"I can do all things through Christ who strengthens me."
– Philippians 4:14 (NKJV)

Goal: What do you want to accomplish?
_____
_____

Obstacles: What is keeping you from achieving your goal?
_____
_____
_____

Draft a plan to overcome each obstacle that is stopping you from achieving your goal.
_____
_____
_____
_____
_____

Steps: What small steps do you need to take to accomplish your goal?
_____
_____
_____
_____
_____

Time: When do you expect to accomplish your goal?
_____
_____

Evaluate: Are the steps to achieving your goal working? What is working and what is not? What needs to change? What will you do instead?

_____
_____
_____
_____
_____
_____

Adjust: Make any adjustments needed so that you can successfully achieve your goal. What are these adjustments?

_____
_____
_____
_____

Measure: How will you know when you have achieved your goal? Be specific.

_____
_____
_____

Seek God's plan for you in all you do. After prayer, listening and observing, what is the next goal you believe God has for you?

_____
_____
_____
_____
_____
_____
_____

"I never lose. I either win or I learn."
– Nelson Mandela

Goal: What do you want to accomplish?

_____

_____

Obstacles: What is keeping you from achieving your goal?

_____

_____

_____

Draft a plan to overcome each obstacle that is stopping you from achieving your goal.

_____

_____

_____

_____

_____

_____

Steps: What small steps do you need to take to accomplish your goal?

_____

_____

_____

_____

_____

Time: When do you expect to accomplish your goal?

_____

_____

Evaluate: Are the steps to achieving your goal working? What is working and what is not? What needs to change? What will you do instead?

_____
_____
_____
_____
_____
_____

Adjust: Make any adjustments needed so that you can successfully achieve your goal. What are these adjustments?

_____
_____
_____
_____

Measure: How will you know when you have achieved your goal? Be specific.

_____
_____
_____

Seek God's plan for you in all you do. After prayer, listening and observing, what is the next goal you believe God has for you?

_____
_____
_____
_____
_____
_____
_____

"What this power is I cannot say; all I know is that it exists, and it becomes available only when a man is in that state of mind in which he knows exactly what he wants and is fully determined not to quit until he finds it."
– Alexander Graham Bell

Goal: What do you want to accomplish?

_____
_____

Obstacles: What is keeping you from achieving your goal?

_____
_____
_____

Draft a plan to overcome each obstacle that is stopping you from achieving your goal.

_____
_____
_____
_____
_____
_____

Steps: What small steps do you need to take to accomplish your goal?

_____
_____
_____
_____
_____
_____

Time: When do you expect to accomplish your goal?

_____
_____

Evaluate: Are the steps to achieving your goal working? What is working and what is not? What needs to change? What will you do instead?

_____
_____
_____
_____
_____
_____

Adjust: Make any adjustments needed so that you can successfully achieve your goal. What are these adjustments?

_____
_____
_____
_____

Measure: How will you know when you have achieved your goal? Be specific.

_____
_____
_____

Seek God's plan for you in all you do. After prayer, listening and observing, what is the next goal you believe God has for you?

_____
_____
_____
_____
_____
_____
_____
_____

"In ordinary life we hardly realize that we receive a great deal more than we give, and that it is only with gratitude that life becomes rich."
– Dietrich Bonhoeffer

Goal: What do you want to accomplish?
_____
_____

Obstacles: What is keeping you from achieving your goal?
_____
_____
_____

Draft a plan to overcome each obstacle that is stopping you from achieving your goal.
_____
_____
_____
_____
_____
_____

Steps: What small steps do you need to take to accomplish your goal?
_____
_____
_____
_____
_____
_____

Time: When do you expect to accomplish your goal?
_____
_____

Evaluate: Are the steps to achieving your goal working? What is working and what is not? What needs to change? What will you do instead?

_____
_____
_____
_____
_____
_____

Adjust: Make any adjustments needed so that you can successfully achieve your goal. What are these adjustments?

_____
_____
_____
_____

Measure: How will you know when you have achieved your goal? Be specific.

_____
_____
_____

Seek God's plan for you in all you do. After prayer, listening and observing, what is the next goal you believe God has for you?

_____
_____
_____
_____
_____
_____
_____
_____

"There are two big forces at work, external and internal. We have very little control over external forces such as natural disasters, illness and pain. What really matters in the internal force. How do I respond to those disasters? Over that I have complete control."
- Leo Buscaglia

Goal: What do you want to accomplish?

_____
_____

Obstacles: What is keeping you from achieving your goal?

_____
_____
_____

Draft a plan to overcome each obstacle that is stopping you from achieving your goal.

_____
_____
_____
_____
_____
_____

Steps: What small steps do you need to take to accomplish your goal?

_____
_____
_____
_____
_____
_____

Time: When do you expect to accomplish your goal?

_____
_____

Evaluate: Are the steps to achieving your goal working? What is working and what is not? What needs to change? What will you do instead?

_____

_____

_____

_____

_____

_____

Adjust: Make any adjustments needed so that you can successfully achieve your goal. What are these adjustments?

_____

_____

_____

_____

Measure: How will you know when you have achieved your goal? Be specific.

_____

_____

_____

Seek God's plan for you in all you do. After prayer, listening and observing, what is the next goal you believe God has for you?

_____

_____

_____

_____

_____

_____

_____

_____

> *"Happiness resides not in possessions and not in gold. The feeling of happiness resides in the soul."*
> *- Democritus*

Goal: What do you want to accomplish?

_____

_____

Obstacles: What is keeping you from achieving your goal?

_____

_____

_____

Draft a plan to overcome each obstacle that is stopping you from achieving your goal.

_____

_____

_____

_____

_____

_____

Steps: What small steps do you need to take to accomplish your goal?

_____

_____

_____

_____

_____

Time: When do you expect to accomplish your goal?

_____

_____

Evaluate: Are the steps to achieving your goal working? What is working and what is not? What needs to change? What will you do instead?

_____

_____

_____

_____

_____

_____

Adjust: Make any adjustments needed so that you can successfully achieve your goal. What are these adjustments?

_____

_____

_____

_____

Measure: How will you know when you have achieved your goal? Be specific.

_____

_____

_____

Seek God's plan for you in all you do. After prayer, listening and observing, what is the next goal you believe God has for you?

_____

_____

_____

_____

_____

_____

_____

"If you can dream it, you can do it. The way to get started is to quit talking and begin doing."
— Walt Disney

Goal: What do you want to accomplish?
_____
_____

Obstacles: What is keeping you from achieving your goal?
_____
_____
_____

Draft a plan to overcome each obstacle that is stopping you from achieving your goal.
_____
_____
_____
_____
_____

Steps: What small steps do you need to take to accomplish your goal?
_____
_____
_____
_____
_____

Time: When do you expect to accomplish your goal?
_____
_____

Evaluate: Are the steps to achieving your goal working? What is working and what is not? What needs to change? What will you do instead?

_____
_____
_____
_____
_____
_____

Adjust: Make any adjustments needed so that you can successfully achieve your goal. What are these adjustments?

_____
_____
_____
_____

Measure: How will you know when you have achieved your goal? Be specific.

_____
_____

Seek God's plan for you in all you do. After prayer, listening and observing, what is the next goal you believe God has for you?

_____
_____
_____
_____
_____
_____
_____

"Our greatest weakness lies in giving up. The most certain way to succeed is to try just one more time."
– Thomas A. Edison

Goal: What do you want to accomplish?
_____
_____

Obstacles: What is keeping you from achieving your goal?
_____
_____
_____

Draft a plan to overcome each obstacle that is stopping you from achieving your goal.
_____
_____
_____
_____
_____

Steps: What small steps do you need to take to accomplish your goal?
_____
_____
_____
_____
_____

Time: When do you expect to accomplish your goal?
_____
_____

Evaluate: Are the steps to achieving your goal working? What is working and what is not? What needs to change? What will you do instead?

_____
_____
_____
_____
_____
_____

Adjust: Make any adjustments needed so that you can successfully achieve your goal. What are these adjustments?

_____
_____
_____
_____

Measure: How will you know when you have achieved your goal? Be specific.

_____
_____
_____

Seek God's plan for you in all you do. After prayer, listening and observing, what is the next goal you believe God has for you?

_____
_____
_____
_____
_____
_____
_____
_____

> *"In the middle of difficulty lies opportunity."*
> *— Albert Einstein*

Goal: What do you want to accomplish?
_____
_____

Obstacles: What is keeping you from achieving your goal?
_____
_____
_____

Draft a plan to overcome each obstacle that is stopping you from achieving your goal.
_____
_____
_____
_____
_____

Steps: What small steps do you need to take to accomplish your goal?
_____
_____
_____
_____
_____

Time: When do you expect to accomplish your goal?
_____
_____

Evaluate: Are the steps to achieving your goal working? What is working and what is not? What needs to change? What will you do instead?

_____
_____
_____
_____
_____
_____

Adjust: Make any adjustments needed so that you can successfully achieve your goal. What are these adjustments?

_____
_____
_____
_____

Measure: How will you know when you have achieved your goal? Be specific.

_____
_____
_____

Seek God's plan for you in all you do. After prayer, listening and observing, what is the next goal you believe God has for you?

_____
_____
_____
_____
_____
_____
_____

"Blessed is the one who does not walk in step with the wicked or stand in the way that sinners take or sit in the company of mockers, but whose delight is in the law of the Lord, and who meditates on His law day and night. That person is like a tree planted by streams of water, which yields its fruit in season and whose leaf does not wither – whatever they do prospers."
- Psalm 1:1-3 **(NIV)**

Goal: What do you want to accomplish?

_____

_____

Obstacles: What is keeping you from achieving your goal?

_____

_____

_____

Draft a plan to overcome each obstacle that is stopping you from achieving your goal.

_____

_____

_____

_____

_____

_____

Steps: What small steps do you need to take to accomplish your goal?

_____

_____

_____

_____

_____

_____

Time: When do you expect to accomplish your goal?

_____

_____

Evaluate: Are the steps to achieving your goal working? What is working and what is not? What needs to change? What will you do instead?

___

Adjust: Make any adjustments needed so that you can successfully achieve your goal. What are these adjustments?

___

Measure: How will you know when you have achieved your goal? Be specific.

___

Seek God's plan for you in all you do. After prayer, listening and observing, what is the next goal you believe God has for you?

___

> *"Whether you think that you can or that you can't,
> you are usually right."*
> *– Henry Ford*

Goal: What do you want to accomplish?

_____

_____

Obstacles: What is keeping you from achieving your goal?

_____

_____

_____

Draft a plan to overcome each obstacle that is stopping you from achieving your goal.

_____

_____

_____

_____

_____

Steps: What small steps do you need to take to accomplish your goal?

_____

_____

_____

_____

Time: When do you expect to accomplish your goal?

_____

_____

Evaluate: Are the steps to achieving your goal working? What is working and what is not? What needs to change? What will you do instead?

_____
_____
_____
_____
_____
_____

Adjust: Make any adjustments needed so that you can successfully achieve your goal. What are these adjustments?

_____
_____
_____
_____

Measure: How will you know when you have achieved your goal? Be specific.

_____
_____
_____

Seek God's plan for you in all you do. After prayer, listening and observing, what is the next goal you believe God has for you?

_____
_____
_____
_____
_____
_____
_____

"Think twice before you speak, because your words and influence will plant the seeds of either success or failure in the mind of another."
— Napoleon Hill

Goal: What do you want to accomplish?
_____
_____

Obstacles: What is keeping you from achieving your goal?
_____
_____
_____

Draft a plan to overcome each obstacle that is stopping you from achieving your goal.
_____
_____
_____
_____
_____
_____

Steps: What small steps do you need to take to accomplish your goal?
_____
_____
_____
_____
_____

Time: When do you expect to accomplish your goal?
_____
_____

Evaluate: Are the steps to achieving your goal working? What is working and what is not? What needs to change? What will you do instead?

_____

_____

_____

_____

_____

_____

Adjust: Make any adjustments needed so that you can successfully achieve your goal. What are these adjustments?

_____

_____

_____

_____

Measure: How will you know when you have achieved your goal? Be specific.

_____

_____

_____

Seek God's plan for you in all you do. After prayer, listening and observing, what is the next goal you believe God has for you?

_____

_____

_____

_____

_____

_____

_____

_____

"There is only one corner of the universe you can be certain of improving, and that's your own self."
- Aldous Huxley

Goal: What do you want to accomplish?
_____
_____

Obstacles: What is keeping you from achieving your goal?
_____
_____
_____

Draft a plan to overcome each obstacle that is stopping you from achieving your goal.
_____
_____
_____
_____
_____
_____

Steps: What small steps do you need to take to accomplish your goal?
_____
_____
_____
_____
_____
_____

Time: When do you expect to accomplish your goal?
_____
_____

Evaluate: Are the steps to achieving your goal working? What is working and what is not? What needs to change? What will you do instead?

_____
_____
_____
_____
_____
_____

Adjust: Make any adjustments needed so that you can successfully achieve your goal. What are these adjustments?

_____
_____
_____
_____

Measure: How will you know when you have achieved your goal? Be specific.

_____
_____
_____

Seek God's plan for you in all you do. After prayer, listening and observing, what is the next goal you believe God has for you?

_____
_____
_____
_____
_____
_____
_____

> *"Character cannot be developed in ease and quiet. Only through experience of trial and suffering can the soul be strengthened, ambition inspired, and success achieved."*
> *– Helen Keller*

Goal: What do you want to accomplish?

_____

_____

Obstacles: What is keeping you from achieving your goal?

_____

_____

_____

_____

Draft a plan to overcome each obstacle that is stopping you from achieving your goal.

_____

_____

_____

_____

_____

_____

Steps: What small steps do you need to take to accomplish your goal?

_____

_____

_____

_____

_____

Time: When do you expect to accomplish your goal?

_____

_____

Evaluate: Are the steps to achieving your goal working? What is working and what is not? What needs to change? What will you do instead?

_____
_____
_____
_____
_____
_____

Adjust: Make any adjustments needed so that you can successfully achieve your goal. What are these adjustments?

_____
_____
_____
_____

Measure: How will you know when you have achieved your goal? Be specific.

_____
_____
_____

Seek God's plan for you in all you do. After prayer, listening and observing, what is the next goal you believe God has for you?

_____
_____
_____
_____
_____
_____
_____

"Our life always expresses the result of our dominant thoughts."
— Soren Kierkegaard

Goal: What do you want to accomplish?
_____
_____

Obstacles: What is keeping you from achieving your goal?
_____
_____
_____

Draft a plan to overcome each obstacle that is stopping you from achieving your goal.
_____
_____
_____
_____
_____
_____

Steps: What small steps do you need to take to accomplish your goal?
_____
_____
_____
_____
_____

Time: When do you expect to accomplish your goal?
_____
_____

Evaluate: Are the steps to achieving your goal working? What is working and what is not? What needs to change? What will you do instead?

_____

_____

_____

_____

_____

_____

_____

Adjust: Make any adjustments needed so that you can successfully achieve your goal. What are these adjustments?

_____

_____

_____

_____

Measure: How will you know when you have achieved your goal? Be specific.

_____

_____

_____

Seek God's plan for you in all you do. After prayer, listening and observing, what is the next goal you believe God has for you?

_____

_____

_____

_____

_____

_____

_____

"Victory is not won in miles, but in inches. Win a little now, hold your ground and later win a little more — and eventually victory will be yours."
— Louis L'Amour

Goal: What do you want to accomplish?
_____
_____

Obstacles: What is keeping you from achieving your goal?
_____
_____
_____

Draft a plan to overcome each obstacle that is stopping you from achieving your goal.
_____
_____
_____
_____
_____
_____

Steps: What small steps do you need to take to accomplish your goal?
_____
_____
_____
_____
_____
_____

Time: When do you expect to accomplish your goal?
_____
_____

Evaluate: Are the steps to achieving your goal working? What is working and what is not? What needs to change? What will you do instead?

_____
_____
_____
_____
_____
_____

Adjust: Make any adjustments needed so that you can successfully achieve your goal. What are these adjustments?

_____
_____
_____
_____

Measure: How will you know when you have achieved your goal? Be specific.

_____
_____
_____

Seek God's plan for you in all you do. After prayer, listening and observing, what is the next goal you believe God has for you?

_____
_____
_____
_____
_____
_____
_____
_____

"Perfection is not attainable, but if we chase perfection we can catch excellence."
— Vince Lombardi

Goal: What do you want to accomplish?

_____

_____

Obstacles: What is keeping you from achieving your goal?

_____

_____

_____

Draft a plan to overcome each obstacle that is stopping you from achieving your goal.

_____

_____

_____

_____

_____

Steps: What small steps do you need to take to accomplish your goal?

_____

_____

_____

_____

_____

Time: When do you expect to accomplish your goal?

_____

_____

Evaluate: Are the steps to achieving your goal working? What is working and what is not? What needs to change? What will you do instead?

_____
_____
_____
_____
_____
_____

Adjust: Make any adjustments needed so that you can successfully achieve your goal. What are these adjustments?

_____
_____
_____
_____

Measure: How will you know when you have achieved your goal? Be specific.

_____
_____
_____

Seek God's plan for you in all you do. After prayer, listening and observing, what is the next goal you believe God has for you?

_____
_____
_____
_____
_____
_____
_____
_____

"It always seems impossible until it's done."
— Nelson Mandela

Goal: What do you want to accomplish?
_____
_____

Obstacles: What is keeping you from achieving your goal?
_____
_____
_____

Draft a plan to overcome each obstacle that is stopping you from achieving your goal.
_____
_____
_____
_____
_____
_____

Steps: What small steps do you need to take to accomplish your goal?
_____
_____
_____
_____
_____

Time: When do you expect to accomplish your goal?
_____
_____

Evaluate: Are the steps to achieving your goal working? What is working and what is not? What needs to change? What will you do instead?

_____
_____
_____
_____
_____
_____

Adjust: Make any adjustments needed so that you can successfully achieve your goal. What are these adjustments?

_____
_____
_____
_____

Measure: How will you know when you have achieved your goal? Be specific.

_____
_____
_____

Seek God's plan for you in all you do. After prayer, listening and observing, what is the next goal you believe God has for you?

_____
_____
_____
_____
_____
_____
_____

> *"Failure will never overtake me if my determination*
> *to succeed is strong enough."*
> *– Og Mandino*

Goal: What do you want to accomplish?

_____

_____

Obstacles: What is keeping you from achieving your goal?

_____

_____

_____

Draft a plan to overcome each obstacle that is stopping you from achieving your goal.

_____

_____

_____

_____

_____

Steps: What small steps do you need to take to accomplish your goal?

_____

_____

_____

_____

_____

Time: When do you expect to accomplish your goal?

_____

_____

Evaluate: Are the steps to achieving your goal working? What is working and what is not? What needs to change? What will you do instead?

_____
_____
_____
_____
_____
_____

Adjust: Make any adjustments needed so that you can successfully achieve your goal. What are these adjustments?

_____
_____
_____
_____

Measure: How will you know when you have achieved your goal? Be specific.

_____
_____
_____

Seek God's plan for you in all you do. After prayer, listening and observing, what is the next goal you believe God has for you?

_____
_____
_____
_____
_____
_____
_____

"You cannot have a positive life and a negative mind."
– Joyce Meyer

Goal: What do you want to accomplish?
_____
_____

Obstacles: What is keeping you from achieving your goal?
_____
_____
_____

Draft a plan to overcome each obstacle that is stopping you from achieving your goal.
_____
_____
_____
_____
_____
_____

Steps: What small steps do you need to take to accomplish your goal?
_____
_____
_____
_____
_____
_____

Time: When do you expect to accomplish your goal?
_____
_____

Evaluate: Are the steps to achieving your goal working? What is working and what is not? What needs to change? What will you do instead?

_____
_____
_____
_____
_____
_____

Adjust: Make any adjustments needed so that you can successfully achieve your goal. What are these adjustments?

_____
_____
_____
_____

Measure: How will you know when you have achieved your goal? Be specific.

_____
_____
_____

Seek God's plan for you in all you do. After prayer, listening and observing, what is the next goal you believe God has for you?

_____
_____
_____
_____
_____
_____
_____

"We think sometimes that poverty is only being hungry, naked and homeless. The poverty of being unwanted, unloved and uncared for is the greatest poverty. We must start in our own homes to remedy this kind of poverty."
– Mother Theresa

Goal: What do you want to accomplish?
_____
_____

Obstacles: What is keeping you from achieving your goal?
_____
_____
_____

Draft a plan to overcome each obstacle that is stopping you from achieving your goal.
_____
_____
_____
_____
_____
_____

Steps: What small steps do you need to take to accomplish your goal?
_____
_____
_____
_____
_____

Time: When do you expect to accomplish your goal?
_____
_____

Evaluate: Are the steps to achieving your goal working? What is working and what is not? What needs to change? What will you do instead?

_____
_____
_____
_____
_____
_____

Adjust: Make any adjustments needed so that you can successfully achieve your goal. What are these adjustments?

_____
_____
_____
_____

Measure: How will you know when you have achieved your goal? Be specific.

_____
_____
_____

Seek God's plan for you in all you do. After prayer, listening and observing, what is the next goal you believe God has for you?

_____
_____
_____
_____
_____
_____
_____
_____

> *"How you think about a problem is more important than the problem itself. So always think positively."*
> *– Norman Vincent Peale*

Goal: What do you want to accomplish?

_____

_____

Obstacles: What is keeping you from achieving your goal?

_____

_____

_____

Draft a plan to overcome each obstacle that is stopping you from achieving your goal.

_____

_____

_____

_____

_____

Steps: What small steps do you need to take to accomplish your goal?

_____

_____

_____

_____

_____

Time: When do you expect to accomplish your goal?

_____

_____

Evaluate: Are the steps to achieving your goal working? What is working and what is not? What needs to change? What will you do instead?

_____

_____

_____

_____

_____

_____

Adjust: Make any adjustments needed so that you can successfully achieve your goal. What are these adjustments?

_____

_____

_____

_____

Measure: How will you know when you have achieved your goal? Be specific.

_____

_____

_____

Seek God's plan for you in all you do. After prayer, listening and observing, what is the next goal you believe God has for you?

_____

_____

_____

_____

_____

_____

_____

_____

"You gain strength, courage, and confidence by every experience in which you really stop to look fear in the face."
– Eleanor Roosevelt

Goal: What do you want to accomplish?
_____
_____

Obstacles: What is keeping you from achieving your goal?
_____
_____
_____

Draft a plan to overcome each obstacle that is stopping you from achieving your goal.
_____
_____
_____
_____
_____
_____

Steps: What small steps do you need to take to accomplish your goal?
_____
_____
_____
_____
_____
_____

Time: When do you expect to accomplish your goal?
_____
_____

Evaluate: Are the steps to achieving your goal working? What is working and what is not? What needs to change? What will you do instead?

_____
_____
_____
_____
_____
_____

Adjust: Make any adjustments needed so that you can successfully achieve your goal. What are these adjustments?

_____
_____
_____

Measure: How will you know when you have achieved your goal? Be specific.

_____
_____

Seek God's plan for you in all you do. After prayer, listening and observing, what is the next goal you believe God has for you?

_____
_____
_____
_____
_____
_____
_____

"So, do not fear, for I am with you; do not be dismayed, for I am your God. I will strengthen you and help you; I will uphold you with my righteous right hand."
— Isaiah 41:10 **(NIV)**

Goal: What do you want to accomplish?

_____

_____

Obstacles: What is keeping you from achieving your goal?

_____

_____

_____

Draft a plan to overcome each obstacle that is stopping you from achieving your goal.

_____

_____

_____

_____

_____

_____

Steps: What small steps do you need to take to accomplish your goal?

_____

_____

_____

_____

_____

Time: When do you expect to accomplish your goal?

_____

_____

Evaluate: Are the steps to achieving your goal working? What is working and what is not? What needs to change? What will you do instead?

_____
_____
_____
_____
_____
_____

Adjust: Make any adjustments needed so that you can successfully achieve your goal. What are these adjustments?

_____
_____
_____

Measure: How will you know when you have achieved your goal? Be specific.

_____
_____
_____

Seek God's plan for you in all you do. After prayer, listening and observing, what is the next goal you believe God has for you?

_____
_____
_____
_____
_____
_____
_____

> *"The only limit to our realization of tomorrow*
> *will be our doubts of today."*
> *– Franklin D. Roosevelt*

Goal: What do you want to accomplish?

_____

_____

Obstacles: What is keeping you from achieving your goal?

_____

_____

_____

Draft a plan to overcome each obstacle that is stopping you from achieving your goal.

_____

_____

_____

_____

_____

_____

Steps: What small steps do you need to take to accomplish your goal?

_____

_____

_____

_____

_____

Time: When do you expect to accomplish your goal?

_____

_____

Evaluate: Are the steps to achieving your goal working? What is working and what is not? What needs to change? What will you do instead?

_____
_____
_____
_____
_____

Adjust: Make any adjustments needed so that you can successfully achieve your goal. What are these adjustments?

_____
_____
_____
_____

Measure: How will you know when you have achieved your goal? Be specific.

_____
_____
_____

Seek God's plan for you in all you do. After prayer, listening and observing, what is the next goal you believe God has for you?

_____
_____
_____
_____
_____
_____
_____
_____

> *"The conditions of conquest are always easy. We have but to toil awhile, endure awhile, believe always, and never turn back."*
> *- Seneca*

Goal: What do you want to accomplish?

_____
_____

Obstacles: What is keeping you from achieving your goal?

_____
_____
_____

Draft a plan to overcome each obstacle that is stopping you from achieving your goal.

_____
_____
_____
_____
_____
_____

Steps: What small steps do you need to take to accomplish your goal?

_____
_____
_____
_____
_____

Time: When do you expect to accomplish your goal?

_____
_____

Evaluate: Are the steps to achieving your goal working? What is working and what is not? What needs to change? What will you do instead?

___

Adjust: Make any adjustments needed so that you can successfully achieve your goal. What are these adjustments?

___

Measure: How will you know when you have achieved your goal? Be specific.

___

Seek God's plan for you in all you do. After prayer, listening and observing, what is the next goal you believe God has for you?

___

> *"Start by doing what's necessary, then do what's possible; and suddenly you are doing the impossible."*
> *– Saint Francis of Assisi*

Goal: What do you want to accomplish?

_____
_____

Obstacles: What is keeping you from achieving your goal?

_____
_____
_____

Draft a plan to overcome each obstacle that is stopping you from achieving your goal.

_____
_____
_____
_____
_____

Steps: What small steps do you need to take to accomplish your goal?

_____
_____
_____
_____
_____

Time: When do you expect to accomplish your goal?

_____
_____

Evaluate: Are the steps to achieving your goal working? What is working and what is not? What needs to change? What will you do instead?

_____

Adjust: Make any adjustments needed so that you can successfully achieve your goal. What are these adjustments?

_____

Measure: How will you know when you have achieved your goal? Be specific.

_____

Seek God's plan for you in all you do. After prayer, listening and observing, what is the next goal you believe God has for you?

_____

"Good, better, best. Never let it rest. 'Till your good is better and your better is best."
– Saint Jerome

Goal: What do you want to accomplish?
_____
_____

Obstacles: What is keeping you from achieving your goal?
_____
_____
_____

Draft a plan to overcome each obstacle that is stopping you from achieving your goal.
_____
_____
_____
_____
_____
_____

Steps: What small steps do you need to take to accomplish your goal?
_____
_____
_____
_____

Time: When do you expect to accomplish your goal?
_____
_____

Evaluate: Are the steps to achieving your goal working? What is working and what is not? What needs to change? What will you do instead?

_____

_____

_____

_____

_____

Adjust: Make any adjustments needed so that you can successfully achieve your goal. What are these adjustments?

_____

_____

_____

Measure: How will you know when you have achieved your goal? Be specific.

_____

_____

Seek God's plan for you in all you do. After prayer, listening and observing, what is the next goal you believe God has for you?

_____

_____

_____

_____

_____

_____

*"Each of us has a fire in our hearts for something.
It's our goal in life to find it and keep it."*
— Mary Lou Retton

Goal: What do you want to accomplish?
_____
_____

Obstacles: What is keeping you from achieving your goal?
_____
_____
_____

Draft a plan to overcome each obstacle that is stopping you from achieving your goal.
_____
_____
_____
_____
_____

Steps: What small steps do you need to take to accomplish your goal?
_____
_____
_____
_____
_____

Time: When do you expect to accomplish your goal?
_____
_____

Evaluate: Are the steps to achieving your goal working? What is working and what is not? What needs to change? What will you do instead?

_____
_____
_____
_____
_____
_____

Adjust: Make any adjustments needed so that you can successfully achieve your goal. What are these adjustments?

_____
_____
_____
_____

Measure: How will you know when you have achieved your goal? Be specific.

_____
_____
_____

Seek God's plan for you in all you do. After prayer, listening and observing, what is the next goal you believe God has for you?

_____
_____
_____
_____
_____
_____
_____
_____

"Men are born to succeed, not to fail."
— Henry David Thoreau

Goal: What do you want to accomplish?
_____
_____

Obstacles: What is keeping you from achieving your goal?
_____
_____
_____

Draft a plan to overcome each obstacle that is stopping you from achieving your goal.
_____
_____
_____
_____
_____

Steps: What small steps do you need to take to accomplish your goal?
_____
_____
_____
_____

Time: When do you expect to accomplish your goal?
_____
_____

Evaluate: Are the steps to achieving your goal working? What is working and what is not? What needs to change? What will you do instead?

_____
_____
_____
_____
_____

Adjust: Make any adjustments needed so that you can successfully achieve your goal. What are these adjustments?

_____
_____
_____

Measure: How will you know when you have achieved your goal? Be specific.

_____
_____
_____

Seek God's plan for you in all you do. After prayer, listening and observing, what is the next goal you believe God has for you?

_____
_____
_____
_____
_____
_____

"The secret to getting ahead is getting started."
– Mark Twain

Goal: What do you want to accomplish?
_____
_____

Obstacles: What is keeping you from achieving your goal?
_____
_____
_____

Draft a plan to overcome each obstacle that is stopping you from achieving your goal.
_____
_____
_____
_____
_____

Steps: What small steps do you need to take to accomplish your goal?
_____
_____
_____
_____
_____

Time: When do you expect to accomplish your goal?
_____
_____

Evaluate: Are the steps to achieving your goal working? What is working and what is not? What needs to change? What will you do instead?

_____

_____

_____

_____

_____

Adjust: Make any adjustments needed so that you can successfully achieve your goal. What are these adjustments?

_____

_____

_____

Measure: How will you know when you have achieved your goal? Be specific.

_____

_____

Seek God's plan for you in all you do. After prayer, listening and observing, what is the next goal you believe God has for you?

_____

_____

_____

_____

_____

_____

_____

"I am still determined to be cheerful and happy, in whatever situation I may be; for I have also learned from experience that the greater part of our happiness or misery depends upon our dispositions, and not upon our circumstances."
– Martha Washington

Goal: What do you want to accomplish?
_____
_____

Obstacles: What is keeping you from achieving your goal?
_____
_____
_____

Draft a plan to overcome each obstacle that is stopping you from achieving your goal.
_____
_____
_____
_____
_____
_____

Steps: What small steps do you need to take to accomplish your goal?
_____
_____
_____
_____
_____

Time: When do you expect to accomplish your goal?
_____
_____

Evaluate: Are the steps to achieving your goal working? What is working and what is not? What needs to change? What will you do instead?

_____
_____
_____
_____
_____

Adjust: Make any adjustments needed so that you can successfully achieve your goal. What are these adjustments?

_____
_____
_____

Measure: How will you know when you have achieved your goal? Be specific.

_____
_____
_____

Seek God's plan for you in all you do. After prayer, listening and observing, what is the next goal you believe God has for you?

_____
_____
_____
_____
_____
_____
_____

> *"The foundation stones for a balanced success are honesty, character, integrity, faith, love, and loyalty."*
> *– Zig Ziglar*

Goal: What do you want to accomplish?
_____
_____

Obstacles: What is keeping you from achieving your goal?
_____
_____
_____

Draft a plan to overcome each obstacle that is stopping you from achieving your goal.
_____
_____
_____
_____
_____

Steps: What small steps do you need to take to accomplish your goal?
_____
_____
_____
_____
_____

Time: When do you expect to accomplish your goal?
_____
_____

Evaluate: Are the steps to achieving your goal working? What is working and what is not? What needs to change? What will you do instead?

_____
_____
_____
_____
_____
_____

Adjust: Make any adjustments needed so that you can successfully achieve your goal. What are these adjustments?

_____
_____
_____
_____

Measure: How will you know when you have achieved your goal? Be specific.

_____
_____
_____

Seek God's plan for you in all you do. After prayer, listening and observing, what is the next goal you believe God has for you?

_____
_____
_____
_____
_____
_____
_____
_____

"Do not let what you cannot do interfere with what you can do."
— John Wooden

Goal: What do you want to accomplish?
_____
_____

Obstacles: What is keeping you from achieving your goal?
_____
_____
_____

Draft a plan to overcome each obstacle that is stopping you from achieving your goal.
_____
_____
_____
_____
_____

Steps: What small steps do you need to take to accomplish your goal?
_____
_____
_____
_____
_____

Time: When do you expect to accomplish your goal?
_____
_____

Evaluate: Are the steps to achieving your goal working? What is working and what is not? What needs to change? What will you do instead?

_____

_____

_____

_____

_____

Adjust: Make any adjustments needed so that you can successfully achieve your goal. What are these adjustments?

_____

_____

_____

Measure: How will you know when you have achieved your goal? Be specific.

_____

_____

Seek God's plan for you in all you do. After prayer, listening and observing, what is the next goal you believe God has for you?

_____

_____

_____

_____

_____

_____

> *"You are never too old to set a new goal or*
> *to dream a new dream."*
> *– C.S. Lewis*

Goal: What do you want to accomplish?

_____

_____

Obstacles: What is keeping you from achieving your goal?

_____

_____

_____

Draft a plan to overcome each obstacle that is stopping you from achieving your goal.

_____

_____

_____

_____

_____

Steps: What small steps do you need to take to accomplish your goal?

_____

_____

_____

_____

_____

Time: When do you expect to accomplish your goal?

_____

_____

Evaluate: Are the steps to achieving your goal working? What is working and what is not? What needs to change? What will you do instead?

_____
_____
_____
_____
_____
_____

Adjust: Make any adjustments needed so that you can successfully achieve your goal. What are these adjustments?

_____
_____
_____

Measure: How will you know when you have achieved your goal? Be specific.

_____
_____
_____

Seek God's plan for you in all you do. After prayer, listening and observing, what is the next goal you believe God has for you?

_____
_____
_____
_____
_____
_____
_____
_____

"Whatever the mind can conceive and believe, it can achieve."
— Napoleon Hill

Goal: What do you want to accomplish?
_____
_____

Obstacles: What is keeping you from achieving your goal?
_____
_____
_____

Draft a plan to overcome each obstacle that is stopping you from achieving your goal.
_____
_____
_____
_____
_____
_____

Steps: What small steps do you need to take to accomplish your goal?
_____
_____
_____
_____
_____
_____

Time: When do you expect to accomplish your goal?
_____
_____

Evaluate: Are the steps to achieving your goal working? What is working and what is not? What needs to change? What will you do instead?

_____
_____
_____
_____
_____

Adjust: Make any adjustments needed so that you can successfully achieve your goal. What are these adjustments?

_____
_____
_____

Measure: How will you know when you have achieved your goal? Be specific.

_____
_____

Seek God's plan for you in all you do. After prayer, listening and observing, what is the next goal you believe God has for you?

_____
_____
_____
_____
_____
_____

"But seek first His kingdom and His righteousness, and all these things will be given to you as well."
– Mathew 6:33 (NIV)

Goal: What do you want to accomplish?

_____
_____

Obstacles: What is keeping you from achieving your goal?

_____
_____
_____

Draft a plan to overcome each obstacle that is stopping you from achieving your goal.

_____
_____
_____
_____
_____
_____

Steps: What small steps do you need to take to accomplish your goal?

_____
_____
_____
_____
_____

Time: When do you expect to accomplish your goal?

_____
_____

Evaluate: Are the steps to achieving your goal working? What is working and what is not? What needs to change? What will you do instead?

_____
_____
_____
_____
_____
_____

Adjust: Make any adjustments needed so that you can successfully achieve your goal. What are these adjustments?

_____
_____
_____
_____

Measure: How will you know when you have achieved your goal? Be specific.

_____
_____
_____

Seek God's plan for you in all you do. After prayer, listening and observing, what is the next goal you believe God has for you?

_____
_____
_____
_____
_____
_____
_____
_____

"And we know that in all things God works for the good of those who love Him, who have been called according to His purpose."
– Romans 8:28 (NIV)

Goal: What do you want to accomplish?
_____
_____

Obstacles: What is keeping you from achieving your goal?
_____
_____
_____

Draft a plan to overcome each obstacle that is stopping you from achieving your goal.
_____
_____
_____
_____
_____
_____

Steps: What small steps do you need to take to accomplish your goal?
_____
_____
_____
_____
_____

Time: When do you expect to accomplish your goal?
_____
_____

Evaluate: Are the steps to achieving your goal working? What is working and what is not? What needs to change? What will you do instead?

_____

_____

_____

_____

_____

Adjust: Make any adjustments needed so that you can successfully achieve your goal. What are these adjustments?

_____

_____

_____

Measure: How will you know when you have achieved your goal? Be specific.

_____

_____

Seek God's plan for you in all you do. After prayer, listening and observing, what is the next goal you believe God has for you?

_____

_____

_____

_____

_____

_____

"Inch by inch, life's a cinch. Yard by yard, life is hard."
– John Bytheway

Goal: What do you want to accomplish?
_____
_____

Obstacles: What is keeping you from achieving your goal?
_____
_____
_____

Draft a plan to overcome each obstacle that is stopping you from achieving your goal.
_____
_____
_____
_____
_____
_____

Steps: What small steps do you need to take to accomplish your goal?
_____
_____
_____
_____
_____

Time: When do you expect to accomplish your goal?
_____
_____

Evaluate: Are the steps to achieving your goal working? What is working and what is not? What needs to change? What will you do instead?

_____
_____
_____
_____
_____
_____

Adjust: Make any adjustments needed so that you can successfully achieve your goal. What are these adjustments?

_____
_____
_____
_____

Measure: How will you know when you have achieved your goal? Be specific.

_____
_____
_____

Seek God's plan for you in all you do. After prayer, listening and observing, what is the next goal you believe God has for you?

_____
_____
_____
_____
_____
_____
_____

> *"Trust in the Lord with all your heart and lean not on your own understanding; in all your ways submit to Him and He will make your way straight."*
> *– Proverbs 3:5-6 (NIV)*

Goal: What do you want to accomplish?

_____

_____

Obstacles: What is keeping you from achieving your goal?

_____

_____

_____

Draft a plan to overcome each obstacle that is stopping you from achieving your goal.

_____

_____

_____

_____

_____

_____

Steps: What small steps do you need to take to accomplish your goal?

_____

_____

_____

_____

_____

_____

Time: When do you expect to accomplish your goal?

_____

_____

Evaluate: Are the steps to achieving your goal working? What is working and what is not? What needs to change? What will you do instead?

_____

_____

_____

_____

_____

Adjust: Make any adjustments needed so that you can successfully achieve your goal. What are these adjustments?

_____

_____

_____

Measure: How will you know when you have achieved your goal? Be specific.

_____

_____

Seek God's plan for you in all you do. After prayer, listening and observing, what is the next goal you believe God has for you?

_____

_____

_____

_____

_____

_____

_____

For More Information

Thank you for your interest.

I would love to hear from you! I am very interested in receiving your input concerning the ways in which Goal Achieving Tools: GOD'S TEAMS and More! has impacted your life.

For booking speaking engagements, information concerning seminars and webinars, or to order more products, contact:

Frances Marx

Your Success Advocate

Speaker, Author, Mentor

E-mail: yoursuccessadvocate@gmail.com

Other publications by Frances Marx:

My Success Journal: A Guided Tour on the Journey to Self-Discovery

How to Journal Your Way to Personal Success: A Guided Tour on the Journey to Self-Discovery

My Success Journal: Writing with a Purpose

The above-mentioned books are available on www.amazon.com

Mall Order Bride: A True Cinderella Story (currently only available by order from the author)

For bulk orders, or to arrange for speaking engagements, please contact the author at yoursuccessadvocate@gmail.com

ABOUT THE AUTHOR

Frances Marx is originally from Chicago, Illinois and has lived in Sarasota, Florida since 1985. To her, living in Sarasota is like one more day in paradise. In her spare time, she likes to read and discuss the Bible, ride her bike and play Pickleball with her husband.

Frances is happily married and is a mother, grandmother and great-grandmother. She is also a well-respected certified counselor, educator, author, speaker, entrepreneur and family-oriented woman who loves the Lord.

She is creative and loves to brain-storm and problem solve with people to help encourage them to seek God's calling on their lives. Her passion is to be a success advocate to all those she meets. In each stage of her life, Frances has loved her work and desires others to have that same opportunity.

Frances believes that <u>Goal Achieving Tools: GOD'S TEAMS and More!</u> is a tremendous tool for people to use to help them achieve their goals. Everyone who wants to work on themselves and on changing the direction of their life will benefit by reading this book and following the guidelines given.

"I hope that my achievements in life would be these:

That I have left the world a better place for my being here.

That I have taught my children faith in God, courage, perseverance and strength.

That I have made a positive difference in the lives of all those I have met.

That I have been able to reflect God's love to others as He has loved me."

- Frances Marx

www.ingramcontent.com/pod-product-compliance
Lightning Source LLC
Chambersburg PA
CBHW081458040426
42446CB00016B/3297